Ants

Ross, Edward Shearman, 1
Ants /

c1993.
33305212954394
la   01/22/08

Published in the United States of America by The Child's World®
P.O. Box 326
Chanhassen, MN 55317-0326
800-599-READ
www.childsworld.com

Project Manager Mary Berendes
Editor Katherine Stevenson, Ph.D.
Designer Mary Berendes
**Our sincere thanks to Robert Mitchell, Ph.D.,
for his input and guidance on this book.**

Library of Congress Cataloging-in-Publication Data
Ross, Edward Shearman, 1915–
Ants / by Edward S. Ross.
p. cm.
ISBN 1-56766-398-2 (lib. bdg. : alk. paper)
1. Ants—Juvenile literature. [1. Ants.] I. Title.
QL568.F7 R67 2003
595.79'6—dc21
2001000295

On the cover...

Front cover: These leaf-cutter ants are eating all of the leaves on the stem of a plant.
Page 2: This red carpenter ant is leaving its nest through a tunnel.

Table of Contents

It's fun to sit in the grass on a warm summer day. Have you ever watched all the tiny creatures hurrying about on the ground? Some of them come and go through a small hole in a hill of dirt. These little bugs are always hard at work. They work hard to get food. They work hard to keep the little hill clean. They're some of the busiest creatures on Earth. What are these busy creatures? They're ants!

⇐ These red harvester ants are busy working near their nest entrance.

What Are Ants?

An ant is a kind of **insect**. The body of an adult insect is divided into three different areas. The front area is the head. The middle area is the **thorax**, or chest. The back area is the **abdomen**, or stomach region. Most insects also have six legs and two sets of wings. All ants have six legs. Only some ants have wings.

Ants have big jaws, called **mandibles**, that work a lot like scissors. The ants use their mandibles to bite things, cut things, and even carry things. Ants also have two feelers, or **antennae**. These antennae help the ants find their way around and sense danger. Many ants also have a stinger they can use if something attacks them.

From closeup you can see all the parts ⇒
of this Asiatic weaver ant's body.

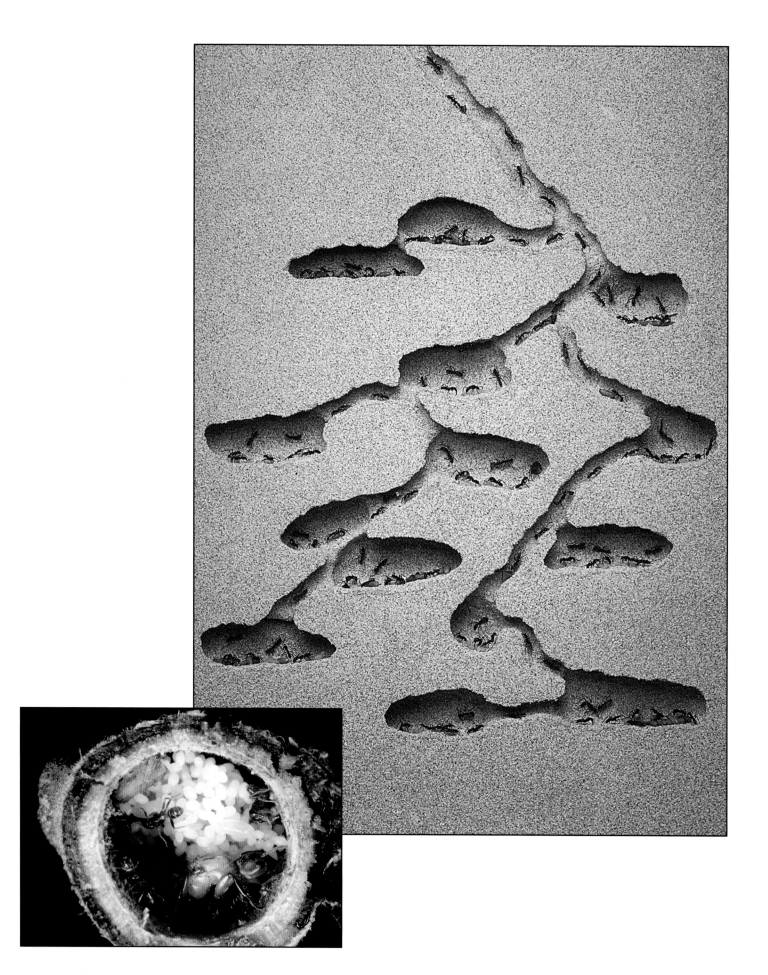

Ants live in crowded nests called **colonies**. Many ant colonies are underground. They have lots of dark tunnels. The tunnels go to different parts of the nest. The ants use their antennae to feel their way around the nest. The antennae can follow trails left by other ants. An ant's antennae can feel and sense many things the ant can't see with its eyes.

Each colony is really one big family. It is made up of a mother, called the *queen*, and her young. The queen of an ant colony has only one job—to lay thousands of eggs. All the other ants are divided into groups, called **castes**. Each caste has a different job to do.

⇐ *Main photo*: Here you can see what the tunnels of an ant colony look like underground.

Small photo: This Azteca ant queen is surrounded by her workers and young. Their colony is in a cecropia tree in Peru. 11

One caste includes males and females with wings. Soon after they become adults, these ants fly out of the nest. After they leave, they mate and try to start new colonies. Starting new colonies is this caste's job.

The rest of the ants are wingless females. They are called *workers*. The largest workers are called *soldiers*. The soldiers often have very large heads. The workers and soldiers do all the work in the colony. They build and take care of the nest. They gather food and care for the young. They also protect the colony from enemies.

Here you can see winged ants as they crawl on leaves in England. ⇒

How Do Ants Grow?

Like other insects, ants go through several stages as they grow up. They begin their lives as tiny eggs. The eggs are laid by the queen of the colony. When the eggs hatch, the new baby ants looks like fat little worms. These wormlike baby insects are called **larvae**. The workers in the colony take good care of each larva. They feed it and protect it from danger.

An ant larva grows quickly. But it doesn't grow quite like people do. It needs to shed its skin several times to make room for its growing body. Underneath each old skin is a bigger new skin. After a while, the larva starts to look like an adult ant. When it is done growing, the larva gets darker and becomes an adult.

These bull's horn acacia ants are caring for their colony's larvae. ⇒
The colony's nest is inside an acacia plant in Mexico.

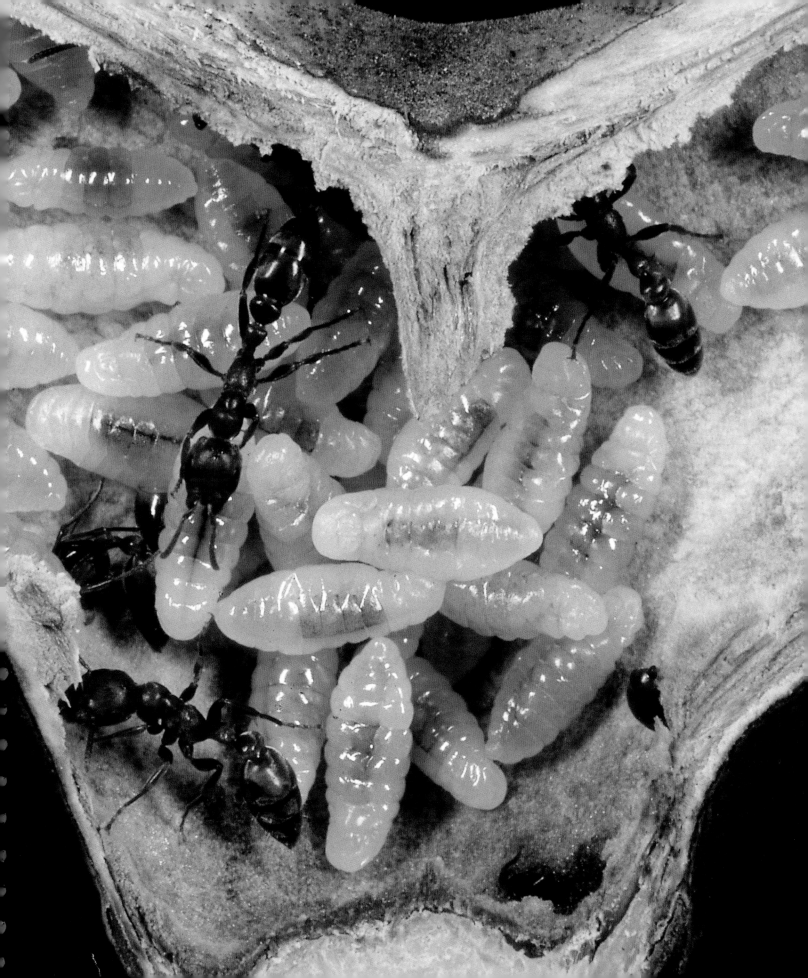

Are All Ant Colonies Alike?

There are many different kinds of ant colonies. One colony might make its nest in an old log. Another might find your sandbox a nice place to live. *Harvester ants* live in desert areas. They use their mandibles to dig underground nests. The ants pile leftover dirt and sand around the entrance.

Plants rarely grow near a harvester-ant mound. That is because the ants collect all the seeds! The ants store the seeds in small underground rooms. They keep them until they need them for food. So what happens if it rains and the seeds get wet? The ants carry them outside to dry!

⇐ This red harvester ant is using its mandibles to carry extra sand away from a tunnel.

Hot jungles are sometimes too wet for building nests on the ground. Instead, some ants build them high up in the trees. They make these nests from tree bark and dirt carried up from the ground.

Often, plants start to grow in these high nests. But the ants don't mind! The plants' roots actually make the nests stronger. In return, the ants protect the plants from animals and insects that would eat their leaves.

This ant nest was made from many things ⇒
found on the forest floor in Malaysia.

Weaver ants also make their nests in trees. These ants live only in the jungles of Africa, Asia, and Australia. They make their nests from tree leaves held together by silk. The adult ants don't make silk, but the baby ant larvae do.

A worker ant picks up a larva in its jaws. It points the larva at a hole in the nest that needs to be closed. As the larva wiggles back and forth, silk comes out of its mouth. The silk sews the leaves together! If the leaves are too far apart to sew, other ants form a line. They pull the leaves closer together so the larva can sew them.

⇐ *Main photo*: Here you can see a nest of Asiatic weaver ants. Their nest was made from leaves held together with silk.

Small photo: This picture shows how the nest was made. An adult weaver ant holds a larva that spins the sticky silk.

Do Ants Help or Harm Farmers?

Some ants help farmers, and other ants are harmful. Helpful ants don't eat leaves—they eat other insects. In some parts of the world, farmers collect branches with weaver-ant nests on them. Then the farmers tie the branches to their fruit trees. The ants help protect the trees from insect pests.

But not all ants are friends to farmers. *Leafcutter ants* are pests to people who grow fruit trees. These ants can carry away all the leaves on a young tree overnight! The worker ants use their strong mandibles to cut out pieces of leaves. They carry these pieces over their heads. The ants form long parades leading to their huge underground nests.

These leafcutter ants are carrying leaves in Costa Rica. ⇒

Where Do Ants Store Their Food?

Sometimes the weather is too hot or too cold for ants to collect food for the colony. On days like this, the ants eat food they have stored in their nests. *Honey ants* have found a strange way to store food. Some workers in the colony store a sweet liquid in their stomachs. These special workers are called **repletes**. The liquid they store is called *honeydew*. Often, repletes are so full of honeydew that they can't even walk! When the other honey ants want a sweet treat, they tickle a replete's mouth. The replete gives them a little drop of honeydew in return.

⇐ *Top*: You can see light shining through the belly of this honey ant replete in Australia.

Bottom: These honey ant repletes are on a desert floor in Australia.

Are Ants Dangerous?

Most ants are harmless, but a few types can be dangerous. Some kinds of ants hunt insects or small animals for food. One Australian ant, called the *bulldog ant,* is large and dangerous. Bulldog ants bite with their huge mandibles. They also have a very painful sting. They make their nests in the ground and hunt other insects.

⇐ Close up, the mandibles of this bulldog ant look like little saws.

Army ants are the best-known "dangerous ants." They live in the hot jungles of Central and South America and Africa. Army ants don't settle down and build nests. There just isn't enough food in one place to feed their huge colonies! Instead, they roam around the jungle floor. They attack small animals and other insects that cross their path.

Army ants aren't dangerous to people, though. In fact, many people who live in the jungle welcome army ants into their homes. The ants only stay for a short visit—to help clean the house! The ants march out carrying cockroaches and other insect pests.

These army ants are walking on a jungle floor in Venezuela. ⇒

Ants keep themselves busy gathering food and taking care of their nest. After all, having so many creatures living in one nest means plenty of work! The ants work very hard to keep the colony well fed and the nest clean. Maybe we can learn something from the busy ant!

Glossary

abdomen (AB-doh-men)
An insect's abdomen is its stomach area. You can see an ant's abdomen very easily.

antennae (an-TEN-nee)
Antennae are the long feelers on an insect's head. Ants use their antennae to help find their way around.

castes (KASTS)
Castes are special groups of ants that have their own jobs. Some ant castes tend and protect the nest, while others mate and start new nests.

colonies (KOL-uh-neez)
Colonies are families of ants that live together. Each colony includes a queen and her workers and soldiers.

insect (IN-sekt)
Insects are animals with three body areas, and usually six legs and two pairs of wings. Ants are insects, but most of them don't have wings.

larvae (LAR-vee)
Larvae are baby insects. Ant larvae look like fat little worms.

mandibles (MAN-dih-bulz)
Mandibles are jaws. Ants have powerful mandibles that work a lot like scissors.

repletes (reh-PLEETS)
A replete is an ant that can store food in its stomach for other ants. Replete honey ants store honeydew in their stomachs.

thorax (THOR-ax)
An insect's thorax is its chest area. Ants have a rounded thorax.

Index

Web Sites

Visit our homepage for lots of links about ants!

http://www.childsworld.com/links.html

Note to Parents, Teachers, and Librarians:
We routinely verify our Web links to make sure they're safe, active sites—so encourage your readers to check them out!